Self-portrait as Ruth

Jasmine Donahaye's books include a poetry collection, *Misappropriations* and the monograph, *Whose People? Wales, Israel, Palestine*. Her forthcoming work includes a biography of the novelist Lily Tobias and a memoir, *Losing Israel*.

Also by Jasmine Donahaye

poetry
Misappropriations (Parthian)

Self-portrait as Ruth

Jasmine Donahaye

PARTHIAN

Parthian
The Old Surgery
Napier Street
Cardigan
SA43 1ED

www.parthianbooks.com

First published by Salt Publishing in 2009
© Jasmine Donahaye, 2009
All Rights Reserved

ISBN 978-1-910409-09-1

Cover design: Francesca Emili
Typeset by Elaine Sharples
Printed and bound by Lightning Source

Published with the financial support of the Welsh
Books Council.

British Library Cataloguing in Publication Data

A cataloguing record for this book is available from
the British Library.

For JK
in honour of difficult friendship
and for his family

Contents

Self-portrait as Ruth

... loneliness, meaning
the ache of thwarted desire, of, in a word, beauty.
—B.H. Fairchild, *The Art of the Lathe*

In every wheatfield after the harvest
you wait for me to undress.
Five men are getting ready to go:
the last round bale has been hoisted
onto the trailer, and the prongs of the forklift
rest on the newly cut ground. A quad bike engine shuts
off; the tractor has not yet been turned on. One heavy farmworker,
hands still on the lever, turns in his seat to watch
as the gulls begin to drift inland and I pull down the straps of my dress
and step out of its little silk collapse at my feet.

Will they talk about it later —
the tired farmer in his loose jeans,
driving his wife to town for Herceptin every third week;
or the shirtless adolescent son on his quad bike,
a collie between the handlebars —
how a woman came into the field
and undressed? At night in their quiet beds
invoking my nakedness
glistening in the late afternoon sun,
will each one think it was done for him alone?

This morning I got up to wash;
I oiled my thighs and buttocks and belly, my
stupendous dark arms. My mother-in-law
instructed me — this is the seduction:
I am ready to submit,
so I adorned myself with earrings and bracelets and anklets,
with the Yemenite choker she took
into exile.

1

The gulls wheel, wait as you wait: for the light,
for the right shot, and the men watch, suspended —
like you, they are about to pass out of my life a little
troubled, changed, because when I straighten up,
stalks of bearded, bristled wheat scratching my bare skin,
and I glance over to see if you're looking,
and you are
then for one instant I will know what I am —
the ache of desire

thwarted. Behind me, the windmills' slow revolutions
change pace; chaff blows into the air
and the men stir. Any moment, there will be nudges,
laughter ... but it doesn't come. One
clears his throat, looks down; another reaches
to turn the ignition, heaving himself
in the seat, which bounces and squeaks.
The boy on the quad bike tells his dog *dere 'ma,*
though she's done nothing more than cock her ears and wait.

I'd have said it if you'd let me say it — *where you go,
there shall I go; where you are buried there let me die.*
But you got what you wanted, and you retreat
as the gulls arrive and begin their descent,
lining up at the edge of the field. Already they,
like the men looking over their shoulders,
expressionless, almost hostile,
are waiting for me, a trespasser, to leave.

Thirst

Atash, thirst, *tzamah:* in any language
an open mouth, a plea; and in *syched*, fluid
sucks out; the tongue — clammy and then coated
and then furred — cracks and cleaves
to the ribbed roof of the mouth, soul
contracted to a longing for the purely physical;
not because it's a parched place
but because the distance between one well
and another, from one spring to the next,
is a pilgrimage.

You, Moshe, *Mashiach*, with your macho
promise; you, *chayal*, with your sullen refusals,
raising a slow thumb from that gunmetal chest;
you, poet, still believing
your language can be something absolute,
that it can absolve you —
violate me, let me love
absolutely.

What you say about us is untrue. It begins with
thirst, when you shout *all right, you want water,*
I'll give you water, and you strike the rock.
We're near the salt impossibility of that fake respite —
can you blame us? From the rock a thousand streams
ejaculate. Yes, it starts with our thirst
and resentment, and then your disgust, and for such
petty rage, your right of return
has been revoked, so why blame us
for the exile?

It's you I want, *chayal*, in your *Tzahal* shirt;
you, Moshe, in your angry dismissal;
you, poet, grieving for your lover on Gilboa.
With all my heart and all my soul
and all my strength I will worship you:
your mouth, with its little heroic twist
from which my angry language
comes. You — poet, soldier, road-builder —
love me absolutely: violate me;
absolve me.

Palestina

My heart is in the east
and I am at the edge of the west.
　　　　　　　— Jehuda HaLevy (11th–12th century)

Eagle, eagle, over your mountains ...
　　　　　　　— Saul Tchernikhovsky

She slipped past
when the border guard
had fallen asleep at his post.
She smelled of sweat
and olivewood. One finger
pressed against my mouth, she whispered:
'Here's where it began — your words,
a thousand years ago, claiming,
my heart is in the east.'

She took off her dress.
Her body was a map of
my body; where she had scars,
I had scars. I traced her terrain:
the ruined watchtowers
where the gunmen had lain,
the wadi where I'd watched a short-toed eagle
soar above the rusted vans, and in my heart I
butchered Tchernikhovsky's
glorifying refrain, claiming
my mountains, mine.

I knew she'd never let me alone
again. 'My womb
is not your womb,' she said;
'I give birth to blood
and shards of bone.'

She lay down,
the length of her body
against my body,
and kissed me
with my mouth, telling me
in my voice: 'Here's
where the Catastrophe began —
your words, your claim,
my heart is in the east.'

Fetishes

The cock, rearing up
trembling and twitching
nubbing towards home

and the anus with its little deceit
that it wants out
when it really wants in.

The *mechitza*, which you can
see through, but through which
you may not be seen,

and the wet redness of the cunt
with its retreat upon retreat
into itself.

At the Western Wall:
should I
should I not
touch it?

Sheba before Solomon

Not that dark temptress, that beauty
pacing across the polished floor, lifting her skirts
from what she thought water, so that you,
seated at the end of the cedar hall, observing her
approach, marked for eternity
silk rising above her shins, revealing
fine dark hair. But it's not true, what you put about —
that she'd forgotten. It was deliberate, as
I am deliberate: for you, god's gift,
setting your trap, here it is, this
flawed body; but with your licentious mouth,
what do you think you're going to trick me out of,
playboy, drug smuggler, temple builder?
Go back to your thousand delights,
but you won't go back the same:
I have marked you; I have made
my own mental scratch.

Israel *v.* Palestine

Hot, flushed, talking feverishly
about 1967 and 1917, about dignity
and the loss of self-respect, the first Intifada
and the Warsaw Ghetto, we watch each other
across a table, sharing roast pistachios,
scattering shells, our fingers
occasionally arriving at the same time —
and two old Quakers are eagerly listening in
but there's nothing to say to them
because this is the private conversation:
a glimpse of your tongue, my body
empty with want, as you stand over me,
your hand on my throat, holding me down,
everything I care about gone.

The seamline

How we desired her,
and now we have her, how we

love her. We followed Rilke's advice,
patrolling the borders of her solitude.

In private she takes off the scarf, the snood,
the clumsy wig. We touch her lustrous hair that only

we may see. She undresses for us alone,
revealing her secret places and pleasures,

her wound. The scar won't ever fully heal,
but it had to be done, this stitched seam from pubis

to breastbone. Caressing the weal with the ball
of the thumb, we forget so easily how the join was made,

forty years ago, clumsily, hastily, without
thought, without anaesthetic, by an army doctor

still in his boots after a short sleep on the tent floor
on the seventh day of the six-day war.

Harry Potter goes on sale in the Beit She'an valley

Yeshiva boys, the Book imprinted on their hearts,
are wandering through the hottest hours in the wilderness,
without a map, without water, in black hats and kippot,
scuffling their sandals, stumbling
towards the border. By midday, lost, betrayed
by their pale bodies and the land they

own, they lie down, helpless, and weep.
In Beit She'an, the shaded walkway of the mall
pulses with shish kebab and ancient frying oil.
Behind the falafel stand a man lifts his chin
at the next customer, prying apart a pita
with one thumb as he waits for the order,
and my heart is peeling open

for you. The report at noon whispers through
the bookshop, and the dyed Russian woman
shifts her heavy glasses and her weight,
looking beyond us, beyond the falafel stand,
the empty carpark. How far — as far as the black road,
does she see it? Yes, yes, she knows the brown sign
to the ruin of Scythopolis, the bilingual sign
for the museum, the Hebrew sign for the swimming pool —

but the rubble and gravestones, from the broken
town, habibi, lying among the prickly pear?
She sighs, looks down at my money on the counter,
drops in my palm a handful of coins, passes over
The Deathly Hallows and so my daughter
spends the heat of the day on her stomach,
on her back, chewing her hair,

11

drifting down to the water, carrying before her
the heavy book like a prayer, oblivious

of the yeshiva students, the border incident,
the boys with martyr haircuts dancing the *dabka* on the far shore,
silver phone in one hand, arms across each others' shoulders,
dancing and shouting and peeling off to begin again
while women not so much swimming as walking
immerse themselves in the Sahna as though it were a *mikveh*,
their dark embroidered clothing
floating up from hidden, forbidden bodies.

Habibi, you have been beside me all this time.
Look, look — even the helpless yeshiva boys,
the old woman raising her hand, cursing
her grandchildren under the date palms;
even Beysan instead of Beit She'an,
if that's what it takes. It can never
be the same, so for whom is my heart
emptying itself of love, but you?

Water

Sweating, dusty,
I step into a shop on Sderot Yerushalayim
to buy water. The man behind his counter smiles
and says, *yes it's hot; I'm thirsty too.*
I could stop for a while in the refreshment
of his company, in the cooler shade.
I could stand here and drink, and drink
and for a moment
it might be enough:
he an Arab and I a Jew,
and water simply water.

Gaza, summer 2006

But still I'll return, and this time
I'll bring a mourning stone
according to the proper form.
I'll start with their graves:
my grandparents, and their parents,
and my sister whose grave is unknown;
one sharp stone every pilgrimage —
for Manos with his bottlebrush moustache; for Yair,
who made this peaceful garden,
the whole commune his garden now gone;
for Rahel a piece of slate from Blaenau Ffestiniog, that
stony landscape of labour; for my unnamed sister
a handful of sea shale to scatter along the northern border.
Each time I return I'll bring a stone according to the proper form,
which till now I'd failed to learn,
and one by one the graves' chiselled words will disappear:
may they be gathered ... the collective life ... 1914 ... becoming
fragments, small windows, and then single letters — *aleph* and *gimel*
and finally only HaLevy's Moorish crescent moon,
the letter *yod*. On every tomb I'll build a cairn,
and soon the whole graveyard will become a mound,
and then a hill, and ten thousand mourners
will bring their little stones — from Odessa and Baghdad,
from Granada and Seville. Over the field where the dead are waiting,
and the kibbutz, the nearest towns, Afula and Beit She'an,
and finally Nazareth, the stones will rise and rise —
in the Jewish quarter and in the Arab quarter,
piling up around the bell-towers and minarets,
until the bell-tongues are stilled,
the crowd chanting *shema Yisrael* will forget
what it was they were called to mourn, and the muezzin will sing
Allahu— and choke, but still they'll come, the mourners,
until Mount Gilboa itself becomes a tomb,

its rare black irises, its iridescent insects undone,
and lop-eared goats will roam along a dusty track from ruined Gaza
to Sidon, from Tiberias to the scattered remnants of Sdot Yam,
so that once again there's nothing to fight over
but stony ground,
as the only thing ever to fight over
was stony ground.

The bus to Ramallah

I asked if his bus went to the Old City
but he clicked his tongue, jerked his chin
and drove on. I walked,
I walked till my heels split
and I was late, rushing to the bus station
at the Damascus Gate.

Among shishlik sellers and plastic kitchenware,
I asked a driver about to leave *where
is the bus to Ramallah?* He smiled, pointed,
and as I came to the stained cement bench
three men gestured to me to sit; three men called
when the bus arrived: *here, here, you wanted
Ramallah*, and the driver smiled and said *welcome*.

I saw, in my hurry, I'd put my shirt on inside out
and now, among men, I could not put myself right.
I hardly saw East Jerusalem, Qalandia —
I leaned my face against the smeared glass and wept,
because surely nothing was worth it costing this:
that we've lost what it means, *welcome*,
baruch ha-ba, a blessing that you've come.

Cynhaeaf

After gathering the larger pieces — limbs, organs, digits —
scraps of flesh are harvested from the scorched eaves and walls
like fruit.

Then they become elegant,
delicate as beauticians, plucking
empty blood vessels, nerve threads,

three fingertips with their unique code.
Beyond the lights, the camera crews, the crime-scene tape,
the conception of survivor guilt,

they search anxious and hopeless
for the invisible knuckle of the neck
from which we might each of us rise whole.

Fragments

i — A photograph by Ahikam Seri

That leg with its red fringe, inert in the street
before a dented bus: when the alarm went out
for the Orthodox body-part collectors,
did they gather him up, did they make him
whole — or, finding the bomber was the only one to die,
did they take off their plastic bags and masks
and catch a bus back home?

ii — A soldier

Rammed, whimpering, against the cracked windscreen,
a blood star crystallising on his forehead, Nissim
scrabbles for the door before the MPs arrive;
New Year's Eve in Oakland, and the lights begin
but for a moment he thinks he's still on the run.

iii — Kawkaba

Habibi, what have you left me?
A sound in the throat
that is leaving my mother-tongue;
a longing for wholeness, or
loss; the memory of a place you've never seen
which for you I'd give up anything
to give back.

iv — Atash

Here in Um al Fahm, the patriarch
locked his daughter in the charcoal storage room
for daring to love.

v — The torture report

When, changing to go out dancing
he takes off his shirt and turns,
I remember the poet's words, and my desire:
dress me, good mother ... and lead me to toil.
In the orange light I touch his scars, which,
Avram Shlonsky — poet, nation-builder —
wrap around his body like your shining roads.

Stillbirth

Flesh-piece, with your gummed eyes,
numb fingertips,
who stopped swimming, who
stopped: forked out on the long cord, you were
purpled, then sunburnt
then radiantly Yemenite.

The mother, heaving at her useless
work, its limp defeat, saw the nurse's face
shut; she turned on her side, foetal,
a failing among the fertile workers
peopling the border. After all,
there were so many real deaths,

but someone wrapped you
in a prayershawl; someone
buried you among the orange trees between attacks,
and, ragged spit of humanness,
you still keep the memory bone
which will not corrupt.

My father's circumcision

Smelling of garlic, of illicit saucisson,
the Marseilles *moel* dusts lunch crumbs from his chest
and mumbles *let's get on with it then*.

With two blunt fingers, he
tugs at the little loose wrinkle
and then with his ragged nail

tears the foreskin.
Briefly, he bends his head
to suck the wound.

My father is intoxicated.
Squalling, impotent,
he tastes his first drops of wine.

Then he is still.

Of this first betrayal,
his mother, patting dry the little cut,
is without guilt —

she turns away from the act
as though it occurs
against her will,

like the *moel*,
wiping his mouth, scraping
blood from under his nail.

Pheasants

They strut into the traffic, resplendent,
each step calculated for maximum effect,
balancing the grand sweep of tail, that
elegant fashion item, a lady-killer add-on.
Dignified, like pub women
setting out on high heels to the lavatory,
concentrating, trying not to lose face, they step
into the path of the car
as if they have been waiting
for just this moment,
as if they have chosen
you.

What if they're reincarnated war criminals,
debauched potentates, short belligerent
dictators concealing platform heels?
Arrested at the edge of the road, uneasy,
they know something, but can't quite
recall what. Are they reliving
a Nietzschean return of near-death,
a confrontation with the flaring approach
of the crime for which they never stood trial?
It's a passing disquiet which they soon quell,
and then from the verge they step
into the road.

But perhaps every time it is the same one
waiting to confront you, when your mind
is on something else — you're planning
how you'll sell yourself in the interview,
what you'd like to tell her about what you *meant*,
remembering last night. This one, now,
will be reliving, with you, your own

Nietzschean doom: you, claiming in eternal return
there's no blood on your hands, it wasn't
your fault; you could not, under the circumstances,
think clearly; you were not fully informed;
that you did what everyone does:
your best. It could happen to anyone;
you were just on your way to work; you have done nothing
for which you may be strung up.
You begin to protest: *They say save a life*
and you save ten thousand,
but pheasants?

The civic centre, Tel Aviv

Beyond the rusting turned-off fountain,
the installation overgrown with dusty shrubs,
papers and leaves blowing in a hot wind, old women
slumped on the old-new seats, a car stops,
the border guards slowly get out
with all the time in the world
the way the authorities have when they are
only making enquiries, and a man, throwing down his cigarette,
rises from the bench, muttering *yalla, time to go*,
and it's almost the same though not quite the same
when in Berkeley two policemen
unfold themselves at leisure from their car,
look around at the traffic, look up,
as though they've just noticed, at the fake building
façades, hands at ease on their laden, heavy belts, with that
sensual grace, that lazy sexual authority of men in uniform,
and turn to slowly stroll towards men smoking at ease
on a bench in People's Park; then, almost like this,
one of the men stands and throws down his cigarette,
muttering, *come on, time to go* — men who as children
were told: *son, never run in public — people will ask
what it is you've done*, as here, two men are being asked
what it was they were about to do.

Lashon hora

To speak of it at all, his tongue
with its seven predilections
and deceits
is to speak *lashon hora*.

Pleating to pour backwards
what it gathers from without
or touching here, *here* —
with words,
with desire,

to speak of it at all,
what the tongue said,
what the tongue
did, is to speak *lashon hora*.

The messenger journeyed for years through red deserts,
remnants, always hoping he might return
to Jerusalem in time for Yom Kippur.
He started among ruined mud houses
whose empty rooms lay untouched, chairs
overturned, blankets thrown back as if someone had
just scrambled out of bed. He joined for a while
the trail of refugees, balancing
bales of belongings on their heads.

He can never sleep: as soon as he lies down
the parts of his body begin their dispute.
Homesick, he can almost smell it, the market on Old Nablus Road,
shishlik sellers out-shouting each other, buses
idling in the dark fog of their own exhaust.
The parts of his body are repeating their boasts,
the scribes' marginalia that the rabbis leave out:

the bowels, threatening to proclaim a work
stoppage — *we're tired of you lot treating us
like shit;* the penis beginning its psychotic cackle —
*it's not even a question
who's in control here.*

But the tongue keeps schtum, keeps
schtum. Not rising to the clamour of contempt
when it made the quiet claim *I rule the body*
it has declared its intent.

At last he stumbles home. Outside the Jaffa Gate
they call *where in the world have you been?*
And he tells them about his journey,
what he's heard, what he's seen,
but the rabbis say you must not

listen to a loosened tongue: even the desire
to hear of what his tongue said, what his tongue
did, with its seven predilections and deceits,
is to commit *lashon hora.*

A stoning

Abraham, offered
Hebron by his new neighbours,
insisted nevertheless on paying 400
Old Israeli Shekels.
In the ruins, a farmer rises
from the ochre soil
after the febrile women
knocked him down,
but still my people are throwing stones,
and he stands, swaying;
then his legs slacken
and fail. Silently he drops
like an empty sack.

Jerusalem performing

I want to invite the keffiyeh seller
behind his grandfather's shop, he is so beautiful
and bored. Jerusalem stages
another son et lumière, a tourist's sunset
projected on the dome, the muezzin's
broadcast across the clangor of the bells,
and a boy scurries across the square,
holding his tallit wide — he is a bird, a boat,
the white fabric billowing sails.
Everywhere that gesture of prayer:
Ahikam Seri's settler, submitting
before the emptied hills of Judea,
the black tattoo of his tfillin
coiling glossy and precise
over his fine muscled forearm.

The Palestine or orange-tufted sunbird

The brewer's blackbird turns on you
the flat disk of its eye, knowing. Glossy,
a ghetto creature, strutting proprietor
of the gutter, he picks decay. His cousin,
descending, flashes red, undressing
not flirting: exhibitionist.

Beyond the plane's wings they rise and fall,
ignoring the back-lash of the engine blast
as we begin to trundle up the runway, eager
for our plague feast in the promised land —
singing *HaTikva* as we descend,
weeping for the effect,

exhibitionist, like Adam, that half-formed man
naming with his clumsy golem forefinger
babbler, *spur-winged plover*, *hoopoe*,
the *yellow-vented bulbul*, *grackle* —
before Tristram arrived
and claimed them at Masada —

and, for the effect, pressing his thumbprint
on the iridescent sunbird with its scimitar beak,
turning it in his unmarked palm
to catch the light, ruffling the tiny tufts
of orange fluff for which he names
and adds it to our divine taxonomy of gifts.

Belongings

You go into someone's house — a poet's, say,
and look at what he's placed on the mantelpiece,
at his old, heavy books. You caress the silver feet
of the coffee table — you do it surreptitiously,
not wanting to look covetous, because you
are covetous. But it's not the possessions you desire —
the carved boxes, the Japanese woodblock print,
or even the white building with its curved
doorways and iron stair circling round to the left
and out of sight up to the portions of the house
forbidden you, because you're only a visitor,
not a confidante. Want heats you like a sour sweat:
to be so certain or ignorant you can make a claim —
not to belongings, accrued over a lifetime
and set out like this in one place, but to the singular
which permits you to say here, *this is where I'm from.*

Gaza closed

In Cardiff, a man and woman
are waiting for the border to re-open
so that they might go home.
In the evenings they walk by Roath Lake,
past heaped nets of algae drying on the shore.
The man trails behind his wife, smoking
and looking at the ground.
A ragged line of geese
drifts towards land; she watches them a long time
and turns away, wondering aloud
if a bird lives a happier life than a human.

Migrants

What is he searching for
that I am searching for?
I have tried to be free of his rhythm.
I have tried and failed to see a pattern
that is not shame. I've pored
over the distribution maps, the lines of migration,
the isogloss boundaries; I've smoothed
the glossy covers of the field guides;
I have listened to their song.
They have gathered on the lines;
I have heard them going over,
going home.

An inquisition

Near Mission Dolores, men are gathered on the street corner
watching. One calls *hola, amiga*, but I shake my head.
The church squats over her whispered adobe interior,
where the monks gave out plague-infected blankets
deliberately, the one story says — so that Indians
would come to the mission for care and then conversion.
Vic Yellowhawk turning over in his hands
lacre shells collected from a beach up near Sebastopol,
close to the old Russian border where the law is a little hazier,
says *only the Miwok are allowed to take abalone* ...

As I pass, the men shift their weight and spit.
Already I can smell my sweat, though the test
has not yet begun. On the bed I am prepared:
a paper gown over my bra and knickers.
I see too late I have forgotten to shave my legs.
The doctor who hooks me up has stepped from the set
of *Fiddler on the Roof*. He has a sense of humour.
Nu, he says, *mustn't worry — this shouldn't hurt
much. So, you're Jewish! For you
my special repertoire of Jewish jokes.*

In the hole he punctures in my arm, the needle,
threaded to a shining cable, crackles and spits.
He tests north, towards the show Miwok camp;
east towards Alcatraz's *This is Indian Territory* graffiti,
west for Ocean Beach and Cliff House,
where women in ballooning black suits
flailed laughing into the water, and afterwards
thrilled through the Penny Arcade. He pants
heavily as the static flares, an electrical telegraph
of the nerve gone haywire, whipping about like a cut

cord, transmitting sharp bursts, sparks, odd silences,
technical emergencies.

I can hardly breathe.
I smile at his punchline, because I'm polite.
Under the hot light, sweat pools between my breasts,
trickles in the hollow of my back. By the third joke
his face has enlarged; I gaze at his nostril hair
as he leers: I am a captive audience. I smile and smile,
afraid to laugh in case he finds me out —
because what has gone wrong
was always wrong and I won't ever get it right.

Remembering Baba Yaga

Is there a Hero in flight, helped by the Girl,
or is it the Girl who's in flight, helped
by the magic objects, which she is told
to throw down, one by one, at intervals?
It may be either, it may be both, but it's really
about the Wooden House on chicken legs,
about the Girl escaping in it and escaping
from it: it pounds along under her; it pounds along
behind her — like artillery, like an implacable
army, approaching always closer.

This is not how the story was told.
Its moral intent was clear, but the storyteller,
my grandmother, tried to exact something else.
Under threat, what imprinted
was not the Old Woman, nor the Girl's good deeds;
I understood already
all there was to know about being bad:
I understood that to be good,
which meant to want to
do good, was a lie, that
even in escape there was no escape;
that the Girl and her good deeds,
like the story-teller, were hollow.

Through the crack in the doorway
I'd seen my grandmother's smile
which never slipped, her head to one side, coquette,
as the Russian émigré with the tufted mole
and the harsh voice, the pale skin and black hair,
gestured and rasped for an hour, for two hours,
her voice rising and falling, rising

and falling. The émigré would bring
dusted Russian chocolates, so this
ameliorated the voice, the onerous task.

Opposite her, my grandmother sat
sipping tea, taking a lipful of jam
from the battered silver-plated spoon,
tipping the cup to her mouth, then again
the jam, which became smooth,
glossy, diminishing slowly
like a sucked sweet.
Her cheekbones flushed; her throaty,
buzzing language became vivacious,
but after the émigré left, by the back door,
in her black wool coat and boots,
my grandmother, trembling, clattered the cups,
the damp bamboo tray, crusted with spilled sugar,
onto the formica worktop, and staggered a little,
gasping: 'That *awful* woman — why must she
always wear black?'

My grandmother never wore black.
She washed by hand her hand-made pastel dresses;
she hand-washed her thick ochre stockings,
and the suspender belt with its discoloured
rubber hoops and buttons. The stockings hung
limp and empty, clawed chicken-legs,
from the plastic clotheshorse on its stilts,
dripping in the green bath. The dacha,
where she stayed as a child with the Count,
was built of wood on stilts. In winter,
wearing a fur muff, she skated,
and she rode with the Count in a sleigh
strung with bells. In winter, his mother,
wrapped in quilts, was given the warmest place,
on the stove.

I saw the Girl arriving at the bone-fenced
enclosure of the Old Woman, the Girl
oiling the Gate and feeding the Cat her last crust of bread,
because she wanted to,
because it gave her pleasure, because she
felt like it — not because it hurt,
not because she had to struggle, not
because it went against her inclination.
I saw the Wooden House on chicken legs —
bony, scaled and yellow; its enormous,
taloned chicken feet. I knew
the Girl was not moved by pity, or by care —
she got from her good deeds
the pleasure of easing her distress.

My grandmother, one hand to her flushed cheek,
feeling her way along the corridor wall to her room,
where she would go to lie down after her generosity,
after her good deeds, after the dusted Russian chocolate —
she was not moved by pity, or by care. The Girl did it
not because there was the question: was she bad,
was she good. There may have been loss;
she may have been hungry, and tired, but she did
not oil the Gate, she did not feed the Cat
and donate the last of her water to the Horse
because it increased her distress.

My grandmother, suffering on her daybed,
the back of her hand across her eyes,
digested duty and distaste,
and I, frowning, listened to pursuit.
It's true I remember the sarcastic Cat
and the smooth, oiled movement
of the grateful Gate; I remember the heat
of the brave, wise Horse, but louder

and louder it's the noise of the pursuit,
the escape that was no escape,
the Wooden House pounding along
on its vast yellow chicken legs.

I forgot the iron teeth — how odd
that the iron teeth should mean so little. Now
I remember the iron teeth, the *mortar* and *pestle*,
the noise of its pursuit — a pounding sound —
and the Wooden House on legs that moved around.
But there is no Horse in the story —
who put the Horse in the story? And I had forgotten
the sneering Stepmother, the weak credulous Father,
the good, dead Mother. I had forgotten the Cat at the loom,
tangling the threads, making a mess,
but now I remember my anxiety
that this tangle could never be undone.
Of course all the Stepmothers
were my grandmother. Of course all the good,
dead Mothers were my mother, the weak,
credulous Fathers my father;
and the two Siblings my siblings —
indifferent or casually cruel, self-involved,
false — and I was the Youngest, I was the Third,
so was I simple, was I good? Is it I,
in the end, who will inherit?

The Girl oiled the hinges, and the Gate
thanked her. She fed the Cat and it stood in for her.
She watered the Horse and it carried her.
What did the Girl do for the Wooden House
that made it grateful — did she sweep
and polish it? The Wooden House was grateful
and helpless, betraying the Girl.
It told her *run — the Old Woman*

is on her way back, and then came the distant
thumping sound of Baba Yaga's return.

The Wooden House was treacherous
and pitiable: it told her, and it told on her.
The Girl escaped on the Horse, and the Old Woman
came humming and rattling like a dragonfly,
like a helicopter, dodging through trees,
appearing through the mountain passes, thumping
and buzzing, unshakeable, always getting closer.
But *reach into my ear*, says the Horse,
and throw down what you find.
The Old Woman is delayed
by what springs from the magic object,
but inevitably, inexorably, she begins
to catch up. *Reach into my ear*, says the Horse again,
and throw down what you find.
The Girl throws the magic object behind her
and the Old Woman is stopped,
the noise of her pursuit is stilled,
but then it begins again. Again
she gains ground.

The Wooden House pounds after the Girl.
She can hear it behind her, like the pounding
of artillery fire, like mortar shells, coming closer.
Reach into my ear, says the Horse a third time
and the Girl sees herself in the mirror:
she throws it behind her and it's a lake.
The Old Woman cannot cross the lake
because she is pursuing the Girl
in the Wooden House on chicken legs —
the listening conveying House on grandmother
chicken stilts. Arriving at the mirrored water's edge,
does the Wooden House wade in?

Does the water rise above its scrawny
yellow thighs and seep onto the floor
where the Cat sits tangled
and sneering before the loom?
The Old Woman sees herself
in the mirror water, but she does not drown.
In all the versions, with their uncertainties,
I absorb this irresolution: the Old Woman stops,
she turns back, but she is not vanquished.
She will try again; she may still catch the Girl.

The Jewish Golden Age

Tam ibn Yachya, ancestor, boasts
and it was I who found this manuscript
and made this fair copy, in this the year
1584, transcribing Shmuel Ha-Nagid's
laments and curses, the brash conceit
of leading a triumphant Moslem army.

Is it forbidden to say we thrived,
ornamenting each other with the sweet caress
of the gazelle boys who arrived
softly at night, their fruit mouths
like the crescent moon, the letter *yod* —

the moon forever crescent, never full — or
intoxicated Ibn Gabirol, the suppurating poet,
sexually prostrate before his lovers God
and Zion, his skin a weeping open wound?

What if we never lost it, this
embellishment, transmuting red wine
or pomegranate juice into the sweet
blood of a bitten mouth, brought
by the cupbearers, long-legged boys
with curved insteps, hairless thighs.

The border, 1947

Here, in the dusty pine woods,
a young girl, dressed in her clean white Passover shirt
wanders away from the group
and under the trees finds a low wire, a single
rusty strand. Stepping over,
she stands a moment, one foot still in Palestine,
the other in Lebanon.

Storytelling

When, offering your passport, you try to leave,
which story should you give? Ha-Ga'on,
scowling over his righteous fringe of beard,
or twelfth-century Spain, when we chose Arabic
over Hebrew? Or your mother, on the phone,
remembering the silver avenue of olive trees

splintering under tank treads one hot summer afternoon in 1946
for the hell of it, perhaps,
or to destroy cover;

but whose olive grove was this
near Beit HaSheikh, when they were still
Palestinian Jews, scrabbling around the old sheik's ruin
for shards they could imagine more ancient and Biblical
than the broken peasant pots abandoned in 1933, when Sursock,
signing deed after deed under a Beirut ceiling fan,
traded the story of the land he owned
for a tale that Jehuda Ha-Levy in the end arrived from Spain?

Even as you face west,
thinking *my heart is in the east*,
how the word *Palestine* is changing.

To a man approaching middle age

Summoned, you return to this desert
state. You approach the entry gate
on foot, your passport in your hand.
It's a long walk from the metal steps
to the arrivals hall hovering in the heat.

The tenderness of return is
unbearable. In your hotel room you weep
under the slow ceiling fan, longing
for what you once loved,
though you have what you loved.

Of your recalcitrant body you grow tolerant,
indulgent. Your eyes darken.
Expressions that were not possible
settle and remain: wryness, affection,
the beginning of defeat.

A kind of *tikkun*

This is the closest
I have come to it:
a ewe, squatting to urinate
at our approach, an empty chapel
in a clutch of melting hail, the heavy daylight moon,
squashed pellets of dung
softening to green; and you,
on the old slab bridge,
smiling at me, shaking your head,
exclaiming *what joy.*

You leave and it begins:
the way your tongue rests
almost in a lisp against your teeth,
how you caressed everything — your fingers tracing
scars and whorls in the wood of an old table top,
while the pub girls pulled strings of tinsel from the decoration boxes
and the old black Labrador padded
solidly over to investigate, lingering
for the smell, under the table,
of you, of me, of you in me.

In the night there was a flood:
I walked around in boots, half-dressed,
confused. I wanted to kneel down
in the foaming water;
I wanted to be rushed away.
All that night, the next day,
I thought I might be
the first divine vessel, just before it broke
apart, too full of light
to be able to hold it together.

Elijah's return

In the half-light, looking down at your scarred face
I am full of my age, exact. I want to make you
an offering — a grave, an accidental pregnancy;

some small death that will make you remember —
something that will make *this night*
different from all other nights.

But when you swim up through your exhausted eyes
and ask *why are you awake at this hour*
a little of me leaps up and dies.

Each day you're gone a part of me dies:
maybe a finger, a whole organ, a limb.
First it goes pale, and sickens; then it goes numb.

Every year as I'm adorning myself for the seder,
there's the suggestion of a knock.
I go to the door. My hand on the latch —

will it be you there in the dark, leaning in,
amused? And as I think of your lustrous eyes,
a little more of me leaps up and dies.

But though I know one day I'll hear you won't return,
I'll leave the door ajar and pour
the fifth glass just in case.

And in the morning, look — the wine
has gone down; the little crust of cork,
of sediment near the rim ...

how easy it is to be wrong
about everything.

An angel is passing

And the silence which falls suddenly
on a group, at a party, a silence that elongates,
extends, becomes something
unbreakable, camaraderie
disintegrating, returning each of you
to your awkward fear, sea-
sick with self-knowledge ...
Sure, when it happens, and everyone fidgets,
looks down, no one willing to step
into the unknown, one of you will cough
and declare, a little loudly,
an angel is passing in the room.
Released, you laugh,
reach for the wine, for an olive,
wonder what it was you were talking about,
but now you've been brushed by its dark wing
part of you is forever crouching, waiting
just before dawn, your hand
over the mouth of your oldest son.
You hear the jeeps; you feel
the rumble of the tanks' approach; god's army,
god's angel; footsteps, muffled in the sand; a
hesitation, low voices, discussion
in a language you don't fully understand,
and you wonder how you can be sure
the blood-price that you paid will be enough —

Glossary

dere 'ma — come here (Welsh)

atash — thirst (Arabic)

tzamah — thirst (Hebrew)

syched — thirst (Welsh)

Moshe — Moses (Hebrew)

Mashiach — Messiah (Hebrew)

chayal — soldier (Hebrew)

Tzahal — acronym for the Israeli Defence Force

mechitza — screen separating men and women in Orthodox synagogues and at the Western Wall

dabka — Palestinian Arab dance

Sahna — natural spring in the Beit She'an valley

mikveh — Jewish ritual bath

Beysan / Beit She'an — a town near the border with Jordan and the northern West Bank

cynhaeaf — harvest (Welsh)

moel — circumciser

lashon hora — evil speech / gossip (Hebrew)

tikkun/ tikkun olam — repair of the world (Hebrew)